CU01082734

Original title:

Sailing into Sleep

Author: Franklin Stone

ISBN HARDBACK: 978-9916-90-712-2

ISBN PAPERBACK: 978-9916-90-713-9

Stars in a Gentle Current

Stars twinkle softly in the night,
Whispers of dreams take their flight.
A river of light flows so clear,
Guiding our hearts, casting out fear.

The moon spins secrets upon the waves,
While the world sleeps, the silence saves.
Each flicker a story, a wish made,
In the heart's quiet chamber, unafraid.

The current flows gently, dusk's embrace,
Holding the stars in a tender space.
Mirrored reflections dance in the dark,
A journey ignites with the first spark.

Embracing the Quiet Waters

In stillness, the waters reflect the sky,
Embracing moments as time slips by.
Ripples of calm in the hush of night,
Nature's soft poetry, purest delight.

Beneath the surface, secrets reside,
Carried by currents, where dreams collide.
The whispers of willows brush the shore,
In quietude, we find so much more.

Floating with echoes of tender sighs,
Embracing the silence where peace lies.
Each breath is a wave, a soothing flow,
In the arms of the water, let go.

Nightfall on a Lullaby Sea

Nightfall drapes her cloak over the tide,
Soft lullabies whisper, hearts open wide.
The ocean sighs, a cradle of peace,
In its gentle rhythm, all worries cease.

Stars take their places in the velvet dome,
While the waves serenade us back home.
Each splash a note, so tenderly sung,
Bringing us calm, where we belong.

The moon casts silver on the deep blue,
A dreamer's retreat, a world anew.
Floating on whispers, we drift and glide,
The night holds us close, like an endless ride.

The Drift of Serenity

A gentle breeze carries the scent of night,
With every breath, we find our light.
Serenity flows like a soft refrain,
In the heart of stillness, peace remains.

Drifting through shadows, we dance with stars,
As keeping our dreams, no matter how far.
The world fades softly into sweet dreams,
Wrapped in the glow of tranquil beams.

Lapping waters sing a soothing song,
Inviting us where we feel we belong.
In the drift of serenity, time suspends,
A sacred moment where the soul mends.

Chasing the Horizon of Dreams

In the distance, shadows blend,
Colors breathe, horizons mend.
Footsteps dance on golden sand,
A whispered wish, a lover's hand.

Stars cascade in velvet night,
Heartbeats pulse with pure delight.
Clouds like ships on oceans wide,
Dreams awaken with the tide.

The Quiet Port of Petite Night

Gentle waves caress the shore,
Whispers float, forevermore.
Lamps aglow with softest light,
Guide the souls through tranquil night.

A sailboat sways, a lover's sigh,
Crickets sing, a lullaby.
In the stillness, hearts align,
Underneath the stars that shine.

Driftwood Dreams and Moonlight Gleams

Driftwood lies on silver sand,
Memories written by the hand.
Moonlight dances on the sea,
Silent whispers, wild and free.

Each wave carries tales untold,
Secrets woven, dreams unfold.
Beneath the surface, life does gleam,
In the stillness, driftwood dreams.

The Gentle Rock of Drowsy Waters

Drowsy waters softly glide,
Embrace the shore like arms spread wide.
Lullabies of nature's tune,
Swaying gently 'neath the moon.

The stars reflect in rippling sighs,
Painting dreams in velvet skies.
In this quiet, time stands still,
Love flows freely, hearts to fill.

Soft Sails Across Dream's Horizon

Gentle winds kiss the sails,
Whispers of dreams unfurling wide.
Horizons glow in the twilight,
As stars begin their evening ride.

Softly cradled in the night,
We glide where the moonlight beams.
Each wave tells a story bright,
Tales woven from the threads of dreams.

With laughter carried by the breeze,
Opal skies weave patterns rare.
In the heart, the spirit frees,
As night's magic hangs in air.

Together we drift, hand in hand,
Embraced by beauty, pure and true.
In this vast, enchanted land,
A world born anew, just for me and you.

Drifted Memories on Cobalt Waters

Cobalt waves lap at the shore,
Echoes of laughter in the night.
Memories dance on the surface,
Glimmers of joy, so warm and bright.

Time flows like the endless sea,
Carving paths through every heart.
Each ripple holds a story dear,
Binding souls that never part.

Driftwood whispers on the tide,
Carrying dreams from days gone by.
With every touch, we reminisce,
In the stillness, we learn to fly.

As twilight wraps the world in grace,
We find solace in the still.
On cobalt waters, we embrace,
The memories that time cannot kill.

Floating on an Echo of Dusk

The day surrenders to the night,
Colors fade in a soft embrace.
Floating dreams take off in flight,
Carried forth to a tranquil space.

In every shadow, secrets bloom,
Whispers breathe through the evening air.
As twilight weaves its quiet loom,
Our hearts find peace without a care.

With echoes of laughter trailing near,
The stars align in gentle glow.
We chase the paths of sweet reverie,
In the dusk, our worries slow.

Floating free on the tides of dusk,
Where the world softens to a sigh.
In this magic, we find our trust,
Trust in the heart, the soul, the sky.

Sleep's Harbor Beneath the Stars

In the harbor of sweet slumber,
Moonlight casts a silken glaze.
Gentle dreams softly encumber,
Guiding hearts through twilight haze.

Beneath the vast, celestial sea,
Stars twinkle with a loving grace.
In every sparkle, a story be,
A journey taken, an embrace.

Suspended in the night's soft hold,
We drift on whispers of the breeze.
In this shelter, we are consoled,
Held close by night's warm energies.

Sleep's harbor beckons us to stay,
As dreams flow in like a lullaby.
In the quiet, we'll find our way,
Under the stars, we'll learn to fly.

Echoes Beneath the Quiet Waves

Whispers gather near the shore,
Softly sung by ocean's lore.
Secrets held beneath the foam,
Carried far from where they roam.

A gentle tide, a cradle's sway,
Dreams drift in the light of day.
Nights where starlights cast their care,
Echoes dance upon the air.

Shells listen closely to their tales,
As moonlight guides the drifting gales.
Ripples play a soft embrace,
In this tranquil, timeless space.

Harbor of Drowsy Thoughts

In shadows where the silence lies,
A harbor blooms under soft skies.
Thoughts like boats, they sway and drift,
Resting on dreams, a gentle gift.

Each whisper caught in twilight's loom,
Finds solace in the velvet gloom.
A tranquil port, where worries cease,
Anchoring hearts in quiet peace.

With every sigh, the night unfolds,
Stories in the dark, untold.
The moonlight paints the world so calm,
Wrapping souls in a soothing balm.

Lull of the Silver Horizon

The horizon glows, a silver thread,
Where day meets night and dreams are bred.
Waves unveil their murmured song,
Guiding hearts where they belong.

In the twilight, whispers blend,
A lullaby, the stars descend.
Crickets chirp their soft refrain,
In this moment, free from pain.

Each glimmer holds a secret sigh,
Beneath this vast, enchanting sky.
A gentle hush, the world at ease,
Wrapped in time's soft, tender breeze.

Resting on a Gentle Breeze

A gentle breeze flows through the trees,
Whispers dance on tranquil seas.
Carrying tales of distant lands,
In soft embrace, the world understands.

Leaves flutter like a lover's sigh,
As shadows stretch to bid goodbye.
Laughter echoes in the sky's wide grin,
Where every moment's a place to begin.

Rest here, heart, among the sighs,
Where all your worries softly die.
Each breath a note in nature's song,
Together here, we all belong.

A Slipstream of Slumber

In gentle waves the shadows flow,
Where dreams alight and whispers grow.
The world retreats, a soft embrace,
As slumber's kiss reveals its grace.

The night unfolds its velvet veil,
A lullaby where stars inhale.
Each breath a drift on time's own stream,
In quiet depths, we dive and dream.

Beneath the Blanket of Night.

Stars twinkle in the silent space,
Beneath the moon's soft, glowing face.
Wrapped in shadows, secrets weave,
In whispered tones, the night believe.

Dreams like fireflies gently dance,
In a quiet world, our hearts enhance.
Together, we find solace there,
Beneath the blanket, free from care.

Drifting on a Moonlit Tide

The ocean whispers sweet and low,
Where silver beams on waters glow.
Upon the waves, our spirits glide,
In harmony with the moonlit tide.

A tender breeze caresses skin,
Inviting peace to dwell within.
We close our eyes and sail away,
On dreamy currents through night and day.

Whispering Waves of Slumber

The waves align with gentle grace,
In lullabies, they find their place.
A rhythmic pulse, the sea's deep hum,
Where weary souls to rest can come.

In salty air, our worries fade,
As night enfolds with tranquil shade.
Together, lost in dreams so deep,
We drift along, embracing sleep.

Anchored in Tranquil Thoughts

In the quiet of the dawn, we pause,
Embracing peace, amidst the chaos.
Gentle whispers fill the air,
Time stands still, free from despair.

Mountains high and valleys low,
Echoes of a river's flow.
Hearts aligned, we breathe in deep,
Clarity in secrets we keep.

Waves of calm beneath our feet,
Moments treasured, bittersweet.
Lost in dreams, we drift away,
Finding solace in the grey.

Bound by thoughts that softly sway,
Guiding us through night and day.
Anchored here, where shadows play,
In tranquil thoughts, forever stay.

Surrender to the Night's Embrace

Stars above in velvet skies,
Whispers of a thousand sighs.
Moonlight dances on the sea,
Inviting all to simply be.

In shadows deep, our fears dissolve,
As time and space begin to solve.
Breath by breath, we drift away,
Into night's sweet serenade.

With each twinkle, dreams ignite,
Surrendering to pure delight.
Wrapped in night's familiar arms,
We find comfort in its charms.

Let go of worries, let them cease,
As the world finds soft release.
In the depths of night we dwell,
Hearing fate's enchanting bell.

Tides of Restful Reflection

Upon the shore where memories meet,
Waves retrace with a soothing beat.
Footprints washed away with grace,
Time leaves not a single trace.

Calm waters whisper to our souls,
Filling gaps where silence tolls.
Restful moments, golden hues,
Chasing dreams that we imbue.

Each breath a tide, we rise and fall,
Listening to the ocean's call.
In the stillness, hearts align,
Tides of thought, forever entwined.

Carried forth by ebb and flow,
In reflection, wisdom glows.
Through the waves, we journey on,
Restful tides 'til break of dawn.

The Voyage of Wandering Minds

In the realm where thoughts take flight,
Wandering minds seek the light.
Paths unseen unveil the way,
Curiosity at play.

Mountains of dreams, valleys of fears,
Through laughter, sadness, joyful tears.
Every star a tale to weave,
The voyage calls, we must believe.

Drifting on the sea of time,
Finding rhythm, finding rhyme.
With open hearts, we sail ahead,
Mapping dreams from what we've read.

Through storms and sun, we chart our course,
Guided by an inner force.
The voyage leads to lands unknown,
Where wandering minds are free to roam.

Navigating the Stars of Rest

In the quiet of the night,
Stars twinkle with pure delight.
Guiding dreams upon their way,
To a peaceful break of day.

Gentle whispers fill the air,
Telling tales of joy and care.
Embrace the calm, let worries cease,
In the starry light, find your peace.

Floating dreams like skiffs on seas,
Carried softly by the breeze.
In the vastness, hearts align,
With each twinkling, they will shine.

As we navigate the dark,
Finding solace, leaving marks.
Every glow a friendly friend,
In the night, our souls transcend.

The Serenade of Soothing Waters

Listen closely to the flow,
Waves that whisper soft and slow.
Rippling songs of purest grace,
Nature's voice in every place.

Moonlight dances on the tide,
Where reflections gently glide.
In the stillness, hearts connect,
With each breath, we feel the effect.

Crickets serenade the night,
In the soft, enchanting light.
Water's laughter fills the air,
With each wave, we shed our care.

In this tranquil, sweet embrace,
Find the calm in nature's face.
Soothing waters, lull us deep,
In their arms, our souls will sleep.

Calm Currents of the Evening

As the sun begins to fade,
Underneath the evening shade.
Calm currents flow with gentle ease,
In this moment, hearts find peace.

Softly glide the boats afar,
Chasing dreams beneath the stars.
Whispers of the dusky air,
Wrapping us in tender care.

Gentle breezes brush the skin,
Inviting warmth that lies within.
Rhythms echo, peaceful sounds,
In the quiet, joy abounds.

Evening settles, stars ignite,
Guiding us through the night.
In this calm, we find our way,
Till the dawning of the day.

Beneath a Starlit Horizon

Beneath the vast, celestial dome,
We wander far, we feel at home.
Stars above, they wink and sway,
Guiding lost hearts on their way.

The horizon speaks with tender light,
Painting dreams in colors bright.
In the silence, love takes flight,
Infinite as the endless night.

We trace the paths of ancient lore,
With every glance, we long for more.
Night unfolds its woven tales,
In starlit whispers, hope prevails.

Together here, our spirits blend,
In this moment, time will bend.
Beneath the stars, forever free,
In the horizon's embrace, we see.

Wandering through the Night's Abode

Under a canopy of stars, I roam,
Whispers of dreams this night has sewn.
Shadows dance in the silver light,
Guiding my steps through the velvet night.

The moon's soft glow, a guiding flare,
Illuminates paths with gentle care.
Each rustling leaf tells a story untold,
In the night's embrace, I feel bold.

Stars above sing a lullaby sweet,
As thoughts intermingle in silent retreat.
Wandering softly, lost in my mind,
In the night's abode, solace I'll find.

The Twilight's Embrace of Solitude

As daylight fades to a whispering mist,
Twilight descends, with shadows kissed.
Moments stretch in the softening glow,
Embracing solitude, time drifts slow.

Clouds blush softly in hues of gold,
Nature's secrets begin to unfold.
Each breath a flicker, a spark of life,
In this calm space, the world feels rife.

The horizon cradles the sun's descent,
Where dreams emerge, and sorrows relent.
In twilight's arms, I find my place,
A sacred pause, a warm embrace.

Secrets Whispered on Gentle Tides

Waves caress the shore in sighs,
Carrying secrets beneath the skies.
Moonlight dances on waters wide,
While the night cradles the ocean's pride.

With every ebb, whispers unfold,
Stories of the deep, waiting to be told.
A rhythm of life, eternal and true,
Nature's songs in the night's soft hue.

Salt-kissed air, a lover's breath,
Bring tales of longing, life, and death.
In the tides' embrace, my heart finds ease,
Lost in the ocean's gentle tease.

The Night's Embrace—A Soft Respite

As stars twinkle in velvet skies,
Night unfolds as a dream, so wise.
Embraces of darkness soothe the soul,
Each shadow a comfort, making me whole.

Whispers of night, soft and sweet,
Cradle my thoughts, allow them to meet.
In quiet moments, I breathe and sigh,
Letting the world's troubles float by.

Sleepless wanderer, find your peace here,
In the night's embrace, bring forth no fear.
Wrapped in silence, visions ignite,
A tender refuge, the heart's delight.

Echoes of the Restful Sea

Whispers dance on gentle waves,
As dusk settles, the ocean saves.
Moonlight glistens, soft and bright,
Echoes call through the tranquil night.

Shores invite with sandy grace,
Footsteps fade, a slow embrace.
Seashells sing of tales once spun,
As the tide breathes, day is done.

Stars above begin to play,
Guiding dreams in soft array.
Water's murmur, a lullaby,
Where hopes and wishes softly lie.

In the stillness, hearts take flight,
Cradled gently by the night.
Echoes linger, softly near,
In the sea's arms, there's no fear.

Gliding Towards the Night's Embrace

Clouds drift softly in twilight's glow,
As the world prepares for slow.
Breezes whisper through the trees,
Secrets shared with gentle ease.

Shadows lengthen, colors blend,
Nature's canvas, the day's end.
Stars awaken, one by one,
Infinite stories just begun.

Moon rises high, casting light,
Guiding all into the night.
Owls call softly from their perch,
In the calm, we find our search.

Gliding through the evening air,
Feeling free, without a care.
In this moment, all is whole,
As night wraps gently around the soul.

A Quest for Celestial Rest

In the silence of the void,
Where dreams and stars are intertwined.
The cosmos whispers, soft and clear,
A call to hearts that long to hear.

Galaxies spin in endless grace,
Inviting wanderers to chase.
Nebulas bloom in spectral light,
Guiding souls through the deep night.

Through cosmic tides, we drift and glide,
Among the wonders, side by side.
Finding peace in endless space,
In celestial arms, we find our place.

Resting beneath the astral dome,
Stars ignite a path to home.
Amidst the vastness, we are blessed,
In the universe, we find our rest.

In the Arms of the Evening Breeze

Softly whispers the evening air,
Lifting spirits, tender care.
As twilight casts a golden hue,
The world transforms, feels fresh and new.

With every sigh, the day unwinds,
Leaving echoes in our minds.
Crickets chirp a serenade,
In this moment, worries fade.

Trees sway gently, dance with grace,
In the cool, we find our space.
Underneath the fading light,
All our burdens lose their fight.

In the arms of the night's embrace,
We find peace in nature's grace.
As stars awaken, dreams take flight,
In the breeze, we feel so right.

Stars Like Buoys in Sleep's Current

In the depths where silence lies,
Stars like buoys float and sigh.
Whispers of dreams weave through,
As night paints the world anew.

Gentle waves of twilight's song,
Lead the heart where it belongs.
Each glimmer holds a hidden tale,
A luminous thread in the dark veil.

Drifting softly, we find our path,
Through the calm of a starlit bath.
Eyes closed tight, we feel their pull,
Guided by night, serene and full.

This tranquil sea, a boundless scope,
In the arms of dreams, we float, we hope.
Embraced by night's tender sweep,
We sail on stars in sleep's deep keep.

The Dusk's Embrace of Forgotten Waters

Where the horizon greets the night,
Dusk envelops all in its light.
Waters whisper secrets low,
Of tales long lost in the flow.

The sky blushes in hues of gray,
As memories start to sway.
Rippling echoes of the past,
Surface gently, shadows cast.

In twilight's arms, time stands still,
Reflecting pools, a fragile thrill.
Each droplet holds a world unseen,
In the quiet, we seek the glean.

As stars emerge, the waters gleam,
A silent serenade, a dream.
Dusk will cradle what remains,
In soft embrace, where love sustains.

A Voyage Beyond the Edge of Wakefulness

Beyond the veil where dreams unfold,
A voyage whispers, soft and bold.
Gently swaying on uncharted tides,
As reality and fantasy collide.

With every breath, the night expands,
Drawing us into unseen lands.
Stars beckon from the depths of mind,
Adventures waiting, undefined.

We sail on thoughts like drifting leaves,
With the night's embrace, our spirit weaves.
Freed from the bounds of waking care,
Into realms of quiet despair.

Together we drift, unbound, unchained,
Where the whispers of magic are gained.
Awake or asleep, does it truly matter?
In this voyage, dreams are the flatter.

Sailing on a Breeze of Cascade Night

Underneath the moon's soft glow,
We sail where the cool winds blow.
Cascade whispers through the trees,
Carrying secrets on the breeze.

Starry nights and shadows play,
As we drift on dreams' ballet.
The world a blur, both far and near,
In this gentle night, we shed our fear.

Each wave a note in nature's song,
Lifting hearts where they belong.
In this space of tranquil flight,
We are one with cascade night.

The horizon calls with a silent plea,
While time dissolves into the sea.
Together we sail, lost in delight,
Guided by love, beneath the starlight.

The Lullaby of Distant Shores

Whispers of the waves do call,
Breezes soft, they rise and fall.
Stars above in silent glow,
Dreams await where sea winds blow.

Gentle tides that kiss the sand,
Echoes form a tender band.
Moonlight dances on the sea,
Cradling hearts, wild and free.

Time drifts softly like the tide,
In its arms, we choose to bide.
Each wave sings a soothing tune,
Cradled close beneath the moon.

Let the ocean's lullaby
Guide our dreams as shadows fly.
In the calm, our spirits soar,
Finding peace on distant shores.

Nightfall's Gentle Voyage

As dusk descends on sleepy waves,
The world unfolds in twilight caves.
Whispers of the night begin,
A voyage soft on edges thin.

Stars emerge like scattered gold,
Tales of wanderers, new and old.
A gentle breeze, a tender sigh,
Lifts the heart, as dreams draw nigh.

Silhouettes of ships afar,
Beneath the glow of each bright star.
Nights in silence hold us dear,
While secrets float on sails unclear.

Through the dark, we glide and sway,
Lost in thoughts that wander far away.
Nightfall's promise, sweet and bright,
Guides our hearts into the night.

Dreams Adrift on Midnight Seas

Drifting on a midnight tide,
Where the moonlight's echoes glide.
Whispers of the deep unfold,
Stories waiting to be told.

In the dark, our wishes bloom,
Cradled gently, free from gloom.
Hearts adrift on waves of night,
Chasing stars that feel so right.

Every splash, a hope takes flight,
Beneath the canvas of the night.
Currents flow with sweet embrace,
Guiding us to dreams' warm face.

Together, we sail far and wide,
On these seas where dreams abide.
With each wave, our spirits dance,
In the night, we find romance.

Cradled by the Ocean's Embrace

In the cradle of the sea,
Time stands still; we long to be.
Rolling waves, a soft caress,
Every heartbeat, life's express.

Shores that whisper secrets lost,
Every dream a sailor's cost.
Under skies so vast and bright,
We find our peace in endless night.

Guided by the stars above,
Ocean's tides; a tale of love.
Every moment, held in hands,
Memory's dance upon the sands.

Cradled by the ocean's grace,
We discover our true place.
As we journey, hearts combine,
In the waves, we're intertwined.

From Ocean's Depths to Dreamland Heights

Beneath the waves where secrets lie,
Whispers of ancient mariners sigh.
The depths hold stories, old and new,
A realm where dreams are lost and grew.

Above, the skies paint colors bright,
As daylight fades into the night.
From ocean's heart, we rise and soar,
To heights where fantasies explore.

The tides bring forth a gentle sway,
Embracing night, releasing day.
In starlit seas, our spirits blend,
From depths to dreams, where all transcends.

Evening's Gentle Paddle

In twilight's glow, the waters gleam,
A tranquil ride, a peaceful dream.
Ripples dance beneath the oars,
As evening whispers soft, implores.

The distant hills, a shadowed line,
Embrace the dusk, the stars align.
With every stroke, the world grows still,
While crickets sing and night turns chill.

Reflected skies in mirrored streams,
Stir thoughts of hope and fleeting dreams.
The gentle breeze, a soft caress,
In evening's calm, we find our rest.

The Night's Tranquil Pathway

Along the path where moonlight weaves,
The world asleep, as hush conceives.
With shadows long and whispers low,
The night unfolds, a silent show.

Stars twinkle bright, a guiding light,
While cool winds carry scents of night.
Each step we take on softened ground,
In stillness rich, true peace is found.

The trees stand guard, a watchful throng,
As nightingale sings its tender song.
In every breath, the calm we seize,
Embracing night's soft, soothing breeze.

Moored in the Stillness of Twilight

A boat lies still, the anchor's firm,
In twilight's grip, the waters squirm.
The sky a canvas, painted gold,
As day concedes to night so bold.

Soft whispers echo in the air,
Of wishes made without a care.
The twilight holds a magic rare,
In stillness deep, our hearts laid bare.

Reflections shimmer, dreams take flight,
In every shadow, hopes ignite.
Moored in moments, we drift away,
Embracing twilight's sweet bouquet.

The Last Call of Day's Gentle Tide

The sun dips low, a warm goodbye,
Whispers of night begin to sigh.
Waves embrace the sandy shore,
The day retreats, forevermore.

Colors blend in twilight's grace,
Stars awaken, start their chase.
Moonlit paths on water's face,
Nature hums a soft embrace.

Breezes dance, a gentle tune,
With the rising, silver moon.
Echoes of a day's last light,
Guide us into starry night.

The tide calls forth its silent plea,
To dreamers lost in reverie.
A serenade of sea and sky,
As day bids all its last goodbye.

Dreamscapes Lost in Serene Waters

In tranquil dreams, the waters flow,
Reflecting skies of azure glow.
Whispers weave through silent streams,
Cradling softly all our dreams.

Ripples dance in gentle swells,
Carrying secrets, nature tells.
Clouds drift past in softest hues,
Painting scenes for hearts to muse.

Beneath the surface, depths await,
Silent stories, woven fate.
Echoes of a timeless song,
In this realm, where souls belong.

Close your eyes, let currents guide,
Into the dreams where hopes reside.
Serenity in each embrace,
Lost in waters, find your place.

Beneath the Waves of Drowsiness

Beneath the waves, my thoughts do drift,
In ocean's hush, my spirits lift.
Soft lullabies of tides and foam,
Cradle me, this place I roam.

Drowsy whispers fill the air,
As dreams unfold without a care.
With every wave, my worries fade,
In depths where stillness is displayed.

The world above, a distant shore,
While peaceful echoes softly soar.
In murky depths, I find my peace,
Where day's harsh call finds sweet release.

Beneath the waves, time hints and flows,
In sleep's embrace, the heart now knows.
Rest my soul in tranquil seas,
In drowsiness, I find my ease.

Chasing Shadows Amongst Gentle Waves

Along the shore, the shadows play,
Dancing lightly, drifting sway.
While whispers ride on ocean's breath,
They chase the light, defy their death.

Waves reach out, a playful tease,
In twilight's glow, they bend the knees.
Shadows stretch with every tide,
In rhythm's dance, they will abide.

Gentle lapping at the sands,
A symphony of nature's hands.
Chasing dreams as dusk unfolds,
In liquid hues, the night beholds.

Among the shadows, echoes blend,
Whispers call, as daylight ends.
Together they'll embrace the night,
In the dance of shadows, pure delight.

Shores of Soft Repose

Gentle winds whisper low,
Caressing the golden sand.
Where tides ebb and flow,
And time drifts unplanned.

Sunset hues paint the sky,
As shadows softly play.
A moment to sigh,
In twilight's warm sway.

Footprints left, then erased,
By the rhythm of the sea.
In stillness embraced,
We find what we seek to be.

Stars appear, one by one,
In the cloak of the night.
Whispers of dreams begun,
In the soft silver light.

Timeless Reflections on Dreamy Waves

Waves dance with a grace,
Mirroring the moon's glow.
Each ripple in its place,
Where secrets ebb and flow.

Soft melodies of night,
Emerging from deep blue.
Their chorus takes flight,
Carried by winds so true.

Rippling thoughts intertwine,
Lost in the ocean's thrall.
Each moment, a sign,
In the depths, we hear the call.

Reflections of the past,
Carved upon the shore.
In stillness, they last,
Echoing forevermore.

The Calm Between Stars and Water

Beneath the cosmic veil,
Where water meets the sky.
A hush weaves a tale,
As the night drifts by.

Stars twinkle like dreams,
Floating on a sea glass.
A moment, it seems,
Time's gentle murmur, alas.

Ripples in silence stir,
Holding whispers of night.
The calm begins to purr,
Reflecting soft starlight.

In this peaceful embrace,
We find our hearts unite.
In the boundless space,
Love dances in the night.

Voyage of the Night's Whispers

A boat upon the sea,
Guided by the moon's beam.
Whispers call to be,
In a darkened dream.

Sails catch the night air,
Wandering through shadows deep.
A journey laid bare,
Where the stars vigil keep.

Each wave a story told,
Of hearts brave and true.
Adventures unfold,
In the night's endless view.

As dawn begins to break,
The whispers start to fade.
A moment to take,
In the memories we've made.

Whispers of the Night Tide

The stars adorn the endless skies,
Whispers brush the ocean's sigh,
Softly call the dreams to rise,
In moonlit shimmers, spirits fly.

The waves caress the sandy shore,
Secrets held in rhythmic flow,
With gentle hands, they ever pour,
Their tales of love, the night bestow.

A melody both sweet and clear,
Carried forth by cool sea breeze,
A symphony that draws us near,
To dance beneath the swaying trees.

With every pulse of tide's embrace,
Whispers echo through the night,
In this vast and sacred space,
We find our peace in soft moonlight.

Driftwood Dreams

Driftwood tells of journeys past,
Carried forth by ocean's grace,
Each piece a tale, a moment cast,
In silent whispers, time's embrace.

The sun dips low, a golden hue,
Painting skies with colors bright,
As dreams emerge, both old and new,
In the stillness of the night.

Fragments of life, lost at sea,
Resurfacing on shores once less,
Every grain and smooth debris,
Holds a story, soft, express.

Gather round, the fire's glow,
Share the dreams of those we find,
In driftwood's grace, we come to know,
The ties that bind our hearts, aligned.

Moonlit Voyage

Underneath the silvery sheen,
A boat drifts on the still embrace,
Guided by the stars unseen,
Through the night, we find our place.

The water whispers secrets old,
As oars dip into liquid dreams,
With every stroke, our stories unfold,
In the silence, we laugh and scream.

A tapestry of night and light,
Stars that shimmer, softly gleam,
Bound together in shared flight,
In this moment, we are free.

The moon our beacon, shining bright,
A compass through the darkened sea,
On this voyage, hearts take flight,
In harmony, just you and me.

The Calm Before Dusk

A hush descends on weary earth,
The day gives way to evening's grace,
In silence, we feel nature's mirth,
As shadows play their tranquil chase.

The colors blend, a canvas wide,
Hints of gold and purple swirl,
The sky ignites, then softens tide,
A dance of light begins to twirl.

Birds sing lullabies to the sun,
As stars prepare for their debut,
In this moment, we are one,
The calm embraces me and you.

Breathe in deep, the fragrant air,
The world awaits its nightly song,
In stillness, we breathe our prayer,
Embracing dusk, where we belong.

Stars Reflecting on the Sea of Sleep

Stars twinkle softly, a gentle sigh,
Whispers of night in the velvet sky.
Ripples of dreams dance on the sea,
Cradled in silence, just you and me.

Moonlight spills gold on the waves below,
Casting a spell where the shadows grow.
Each glimmer a wish, each wave a chance,
Lost in the rhythm of a soothing dance.

The world fades away, like a bird in flight,
Swallowed by depths of the calming night.
With every heartbeat, we drift and glide,
Stars reflect back, as the tides confide.

Cascading into the Waters of Night

Waterfalls whisper, cascading down,
Into the depths where we seldom drown.
Like silken threads weaving a tale,
Each droplet a wish that will never fail.

Moonbeams wander through the silver mist,
Kissing the water with a lover's twist.
Embracing the shadows, they pull us near,
In the embrace of night, we lose our fear.

Stars cascade gently, a celestial flow,
Reflecting our dreams, watching us grow.
Into the waters where night takes flight,
We find our solace in the dimming light.

The Calm Before Dream's Arrival

In the quiet stillness, a moment lies,
Before the dreams flutter and take to the skies.
Crickets sing softly, a lullaby sweet,
As weariness whispers, it's time to retreat.

Waves of tranquility wrap us tight,
The calm before all that dances in night.
Hearts pause in prayer, and breaths intertwine,
The world fades away as the stars align.

A gentle embrace of the twilight glow,
Inviting our minds where the rivers flow.
In this calm cocoon, we drift so near,
To the edges of dreams, where we lose all fear.

Celestial Navigation to Rest

Guided by constellations, we sail so free,
Navigating the waters, like ships in the sea.
Each star a compass, leading us home,
To restful horizons, where dreams freely roam.

Clouds scatter softly, like pillows of white,
Casting their shadows on the canvas of night.
With each gentle wave, the voyage begins,
Towards the embrace where the dreaming spins.

With lullabies sung by the night's gentle breeze,
We're carried away on the whispers with ease.
Celestial navigation is pointing the way,
To the shores where tomorrow meets today.

A Navigation of Dreams

In the stillness of the night,
Stars whisper secrets bright.
Winds carry hopes untold,
A map of dreams unfolds.

With every heartbeat, I soar,
Beyond the edge of the shore.
Guided by the moon's soft beam,
I sail through realms of dream.

Waves of silver brush the skies,
As visions dance and rise.
I chart my course, so free,
In this vast infinity.

Bound by nothing, sky to sea,
I follow what calls to me.
Each star a wish, a guiding light,
In this voyage through the night.

Harbor Lights Flickering in Dusk

Harbor lights begin to glow,
As day concedes to twilight's flow.
Breezes carry tales of old,
Echoes of the sea's bold hold.

Boats sway gently, ropes entwine,
In this port, where dreams align.
Flickering lights in amber haze,
Guide the lost in evening's maze.

Whispers of the ocean's sigh,
Merge with clouds drifting by.
A dance of shadows on the shore,
As dusk unfolds and spirits soar.

With every flicker, warmth inside,
The harbor holds all dreams that bide.
In this moment, hearts ignite,
Beneath the harbor's tender light.

Driftwood Memories Adrift at Night

Driftwood whispers tales of time,
Carried by waves, a silent rhyme.
Each grain holds a story deep,
Of tides that roll and secrets keep.

Beneath the stars, the moonlight glows,
Washing over each wood that flows.
They drift through dreams of yesteryear,
Bringing smiles, replacing fear.

Nights of laughter, moments shared,
The driftwood knows, it has cared.
Stories laced in ocean foam,
Finding hearts that feel like home.

Adrift in time, they wander wide,
Through memories of the ocean's tide.
Each silent piece, a lasting spark,
In the darkness, leaving a mark.

The Soothing Serenade of the Ocean

The ocean sings a lullaby,
With waves that kiss the sandy high.
Rhythms echo, soft and low,
In tides that ebb and flow.

Moonlit paths reflect the sound,
As whispers of the sea surround.
Every drop a gentle note,
In harmony, dreams afloat.

With every crash, a heart's embrace,
A calming touch, a sacred place.
The ocean's song, so wild and free,
A serenade just meant for me.

As night falls, the stars appear,
Their twinkle adds to what I hear.
In this soothing serenade,
The ocean's love will never fade.

Ripples of Rest Beneath the Moon

Soft whispers in the night,
Gentle waves lap against the shore.
Under the moon's silver light,
Dreams dance on the ocean's floor.

Stars twinkle in the sky,
As tides sway with soothing grace.
The world lets out a sigh,
Finding peace in this tranquil place.

Each wave a quiet story,
A tale of love and loss told.
In their rhythm, there's glory,
As the night begins to unfold.

Beneath the vastness above,
Hope washes over the sand.
In this moment, we feel love,
Ripples of rest, hand in hand.

The Ocean's Cradle at Dusk

The sun dips low, painting skies,
A warm glow on water gleams.
The horizon whispers goodbyes,
As night weaves through our dreams.

Seagulls call in playful flight,
While shadows stretch long and wide.
The ocean's lullabies ignite,
An endless, tranquil tide.

In this cradle, hearts are free,
Rocked gently by the sea's embrace.
With every breath, we simply be,
Lost in the magic of this place.

As stars awaken one by one,
The world turns soft and still.
In dusk's embrace, life has begun,
With whispers of the ocean's will.

Midnight Drift Under Velvet Skies

Underneath a blanket of stars,
We drift on waves of silent dreams.
The night is ours, no doors or bars,
Just freedom in moonlight beams.

The ocean sings a soft refrain,
Guiding us through the midnight mist.
Emotions rise like drops of rain,
In a gentle, soothing twist.

Celestial paths we navigate,
With each wave, a quiet sigh.
Together we embrace our fate,
As stardust weaves its lullaby.

Time surrenders, love grows deep,
In this drift of endless night.
In dreams and tales, we find our keep,
As hearts align beneath soft light.

Anchored in Dreams' Embrace

In a harbor of dreams we float,
Anchored by whispers of the night.
The world fades, we take note,
As shadows blend with soft moonlight.

Gentle waves cradle our fears,
While stars offer their guiding tune.
In this silence, we shed our tears,
Finding solace under the moon.

Drifting where the heart feels free,
The ocean's sigh our calming song.
We are waves, you and me,
In this place, we both belong.

With dreams as our only sail,
We journey through uncharted skies.
With love as our steadfast trail,
Anchored in each other's eyes.

Embracing the Twilight Current

Whispers drift in fading light,
As shadows stretch, the day takes flight.
A gentle breeze, the last goodbye,
Embracing twilight, nature sighs.

Colors blend in radiant hue,
Crimson skies, a bold debut.
The stars awaken, one by one,
In twilight's arms, the night's begun.

Moonlight dances on the waves,
Through the quiet, it softly paves.
A reflection of dreams untold,
In twilight's grasp, the night unfolds.

Embrace the moment, feel the flow,
In twilight's light, our spirits grow.
With every breath, we find our place,
In nature's grace, we feel the space.

A Harbor for Wayward Thoughts

In the stillness of the mind,
A gentle harbor, peace we find.
Drifting quietly, lost at sea,
Where thoughts can wander, wild and free.

In waves of worries, toss and churn,
A light appears, for which we yearn.
Each fleeting moment gently glows,
A harbor where serenity flows.

Anchor dreams in tranquil bays,
Rest the heart through silent days.
Cast away the fears that bind,
In this haven, solace blind.

Let currents guide the heart to shore,
Where wayward thoughts can roam no more.
In the calm, a message clear,
A harbor found, hold it near.

Serene Drift of Dusk's Boat

A boat adrift on evening's tide,
With whispered dreams so soft inside.
The horizon bleeds in shades of gray,
As night prepares to claim the day.

Lullabies of twilight sigh,
Softening shadows as they fly.
The water sparkles with a gleam,
Carrying wishes, like a dream.

In silence deep, the stars awake,
Glistening trails on paths we make.
Each ripple holds a story old,
A serene drift, a journey bold.

Let the currents lead us far,
In the twilight, be the star.
Embrace the dusk with open heart,
In this boat, we'll never part.

Resting Upon the Sea of Stars

Lying back on midnight's breath,
Resting softly, I feel no death.
Above me, constellations gleam,
A canvas painted with a dream.

Each star a wish, a whispered thought,
In the silence, I am caught.
With every twinkle, I release,
Upon this sea, I find my peace.

Beneath the vast and velvet sky,
I close my eyes, let worries fly.
Drifting further from the shore,
In this space, I long for more.

The night enfolds me in its care,
A gentle touch, a silken prayer.
Resting here, I feel the flow,
Upon the sea of stars below.

Floating on a Pillow of Clouds

Up above where whispers play,
Cotton dreams drift far away.
Sunlight dances, soft and bright,
Cradled in the arms of light.

Gentle breezes kiss my face,
In this warm and tranquil space.
Floating high, I lose my cares,
Drifting through the open airs.

With each sigh, a feather falls,
Nature's symphony gently calls.
As I weave through azure skies,
Magic dances, soft replies.

In this realm of soft delight,
Every moment feels so right.
Floating on, with heart unbound,
In this dreamland, peace is found.

After the Storm

The clouds depart, the sun breaks free,
A symphony of light to see.
Raindrops glisten on the streets,
Nature hums where silence meets.

Fresh scents rise, the earth renewed,
Colors bloom, a vibrant mood.
Children laugh in puddles deep,
As the world awakens from sleep.

Birds soar high, their songs prevail,
The gentle breeze begins to sail.
Hope is born where shadows fade,
In the warmth, our hearts cascade.

After storms, life finds its way,
With every dawn, a new display.
In this glow, we feel the balm,
Embracing peace, embracing calm.

Peace Awaits

In the quiet of the night,
Stars like candles shining bright.
Whispers soft, the world at rest,
Moonlight weaves a silver vest.

Time stands still, the heart draws near,
In this calm, there is no fear.
Gentle waves lap at the shore,
Echoing the peace we store.

Through the shadows, hope will bloom,
Drifting scents dispel the gloom.
Embrace the stillness, feel it grow,
Find the light, let your spirit flow.

Every breath a chance to heal,
In the quiet, truth we feel.
As we gather in the light,
Peace awaits, a pure delight.

Driftwood at Dusk's Edge

By the shore, where shadows blend,
Driftwood tales of time suspend.
Carved by waves, a story deep,
Whispers of the ocean's keep.

Dusk approaches, paints the sky,
With hues that rest the weary eye.
In the twilight, dreams ignite,
As stars begin to twinkle bright.

Memories wash upon the sand,
Echoing the sea's command.
Gentle lapping, soft and slow,
Guided by the tides that flow.

Driftwood's beauty, raw and true,
Speaks of journeys, old and new.
At dusk's edge, we pause to feel,
Nature's canvas, deep and real.

The Midnight Regatta of Dreams

In the night, where secrets glide,
Boats of thought move with the tide.
Sails of wishes catch the breeze,
On the waves, my spirit flees.

Stars above, the captains gleam,
Navigating through the dream.
Whispers soft, the night's embraced,
In this journey, fears replaced.

Every turn, a chance to soar,
Opening unseen doors.
Midnight's magic, bold and bright,
Guiding hearts toward the light.

As the dawn begins to rise,
Dreamers wake with glowing eyes.
Each moment holds a chance to steer,
In this regatta, love is near.

Shadows on the Midnight Ocean

Whispers dance on water's skin,
Moonlight casts a silver grin.
Waves like secrets gently sigh,
Beneath the stars, dreams drift and fly.

Shadows play where silence reigns,
Echoes linger, soft refrains.
Timeless tales of love and loss,
Carried forth by tides that toss.

Sails of Starlit Slumber

Beneath the veil of midnight's glow,
Sails unfurl, the breezes blow.
Dreamers rest on soft, white sheets,
As the sea hums lullaby beats.

Waves embrace a tranquil scene,
Stars alight, so bright, serene.
In this calm, the heart finds grace,
Wrapped in night's tender embrace.

The Sea's Soft Embrace

Gentle tides caress the shore,
Whispers of love forevermore.
Salty kisses from the deep,
Where secrets of the ocean keep.

In the quiet, shells do sing,
Softest songs that blessings bring.
Every wave a tender touch,
In the arms of sea, so much.

Cradled by the Night Waves

Moonlit froth and silver trails,
Cradled deep where silence hails.
Stars like lanterns guide the way,
In the night's embrace, we stay.

Waves hold dreams, both faint and bright,
Lifting hopes into the night.
Here in stillness, hearts align,
Cradled gently, yours and mine.

Following the Sleepy Current

Drifting down the gentle stream,
Whispers float on every gleam.
Softly murmuring, time stands still,
Embracing peace, a tranquil will.

Raindrops dapple, shimmer bright,
Sunbeams dance in morning light.
Leaves like secrets, rustle low,
Secrets of the ebb and flow.

Oars lie still, the river sighs,
In silent thought, the heart complies.
Nature's lullaby calls me near,
To follow dreams without a fear.

As shadows stretch and daylight fades,
The current whispers serenades.
With every ripple, hopes are cast,
In sleepy waters, life flows fast.

The Horizon's Dream in Blue

A canvas wide, painted in hue,
Where sky kisses sea, and dreams come true.
Waves like whispers call my name,
In endless blue, I seek my flame.

Clouds drift softly, shaping thoughts,
In tousled forms, my worries caught.
The sun dips low, a golden thread,
Stitching the sky with dreams unsaid.

Faint stars emerge, their light aglow,
Guiding me softly where dreams flow.
The horizon beckons, far and wide,
In its embrace, I long to glide.

Each breath I take, a peace profound,
In ocean's arms, my heart unbound.
The horizon's dream in blue so bright,
Calls me home to endless light.

Serene Shores of Unconsciousness

A tranquil shore where silence sleeps,
The ocean breathes, the twilight weeps.
Footprints in sand, a trace of thought,
In fleeting dreams, the essence caught.

Waves caress the velvet night,
Reflections shimmer, pure delight.
Moonlit paths weave in and out,
In starry skies, I dance about.

The world dissolves in gentle sighs,
Where time and space are but disguise.
A lullaby that time forgot,
Embracing bliss in every dot.

Fearless, I dive into the deep,
In serene shores, where dreams still sleep.
Lost in moments, I let go,
Unconscious bliss, a tranquil flow.

A Nautical Reverie

Upon the waves, my spirit soars,
In salty air, where freedom roars.
With each swell, I find my voice,
In endless blue, my heart's rejoice.

Seagulls cry in joyous flight,
A symphony of day and night.
The captain smiles, the sails unfurl,
Adventure waits, a wondrous swirl.

Tides like memories come and go,
Whisking me to shores I know.
Through storms and calms, I wander free,
In nautical dreams, I find the sea.

Together, we chase the setting sun,
Uniting hearts, our journey begun.
In every wave, a tale unspun,
A nautical reverie, forever one.

A Journey to the Land of Dreams

In twilight's glow, the stars align,
A whispered wish, a timeless sign.
With every step, the shadows play,
Guiding hearts along the way.

Through fields of gold, where echoes call,
In secret paths, we rise and fall.
A gentle breeze, soft as a sigh,
Carries us where hopes can fly.

In moonlit nights, we chase the light,
Dancing dreams take soaring flight.
With laughter's balm, we find our grace,
In this enchanted, sacred space.

Awake in wonder, souls set free,
The land of dreams, for you and me.
A journey shared, a bond so tight,
Forever etched in endless night.

Tides of Tranquility

In gentle waves, the moonlight glows,
Soft melodies, the ocean knows.
Whispers of peace on shores so wide,
In harmony, the hearts abide.

Each ebb and flow, a calming song,
In quiet moments, we belong.
With every tide, our worries fade,
In nature's calm, our spirits wade.

Seagulls dance in the morning light,
A canvas painted, pure delight.
Beneath the sky, so vast and blue,
Tranquility's heart beats steady and true.

Let worries drift like grains of sand,
In this embrace, we take a stand.
For in the tides, we find our way,
To softer shores where dreams can play.

The Silent Harbor of Night

Beneath the veil of starlit skies,
Whispers flow, and silence sighs.
In shadows deep, the secrets gleam,
A harbor safe, where dreams can dream.

Waves lap gently at the shore,
Echoes linger, asking for more.
The world is hushed, the heart is still,
In this quiet, we find our will.

With every star, a story told,
Of brave souls, both young and old.
In journeys past, we sail away,
To find our peace at close of day.

Cradled in a velvet night,
Our fears dissolved in silver light.
The harbor waits, a safe retreat,
Where rest is found and hearts can meet.

Crashing Dreams on Velvet Waves

Upon the shore, where dreams collide,
Velvet waves in ebbing tide.
With every crash, a story reigns,
In salty mist, our hope remains.

The ocean's breath, a rhythmic dance,
In twilight's grip, we take a chance.
Each wave retreating, thoughts entwined,
A tapestry of heart and mind.

Amidst the storms, we seek the calm,
In crashing dreams, we find our balm.
Night's embrace, a soothing hue,
We ride the waves, me and you.

For every wave that breaks apart,
Rebuilds anew our hopeful heart.
In velvet tides, we'll always soar,
On crashing dreams, forevermore.